BEYOND ALL BOUNDARIES

A step by step guide on how to be an eCreator and ePublisher

Nasirat IMRAN

ISBN-13: 9798351327921
ISBN-10: 9798351327921

Cover design by: Art Painter
Library of Congress Control Number: 2018675309
Printed in the United States of America

This book is dedicated to Almighty Allah for his infinite mercies bestowed on me and my entire household enabling the completion of this work. Also, to my family members for their unwavering support towards the success of this work.

"A DIFFICULT TIME CAN BE MORE READILY ENDURED IF WE RETAIN THE CONVICTION THAT OUR EXISTENCE HOLDS A PURPOSE – A CAUSE TO PURSUE, A PERSON TO LOVE, A GOAL TO ACHIEVE"

JOHN MAXWELL

CONTENTS

CHAPTER ONE

INTRODUCTION

Life can be very unpredictable most times. It can be full of ups and downs. Sometimes, you think you have it all and the next minute you realize you've got nothing at all. In fact. Just when you felt you've known all the tricks there are to life, another puzzle hits you again and you realize you are clueless. Life can be a horror movie and tragedy all at once. Trying so hard without getting anything to show for your hard work can be frustrating. Especially, when you see people putting less efforts succeeding while you remain on a spot. I had been there, so I practically know what being miserable feels like. Join me on a cruise to discover how you can be placed BEYOND ALL BOUNDARIES while making a legit income at this juncture where we found ourselves in the world of new discoveries. This book will take you along the pathway leading to this same door I found. Take literal hands and come on a journey with me. A Journey to the AMAZON KINDLE PUBLISHING SPACE.

These days, it appears as if the future is not certain for a common man. The economy of the entire world is melting down particularly since the outbreak of COVID – 19. In Africa the heat is much and worst in Nigeria in particular. However, there are still opportunities flying all around us. But they may not be easily discovered because they are encoded around the digital sphere of this century. This book has been carefully detailed to provide you with the information that will help you to break all boundaries through exploit in the amazon market place.

CHAPTER TWO

THE CONCEPT "WRITING"

During our forefathers' days, writings were made on rocks and proceeded to animal skins. Classically, publishing refers to getting an author's piece of writing into the hands of an audience by transforming it into either books or eBooks. The author was required to register his ideas into a book and find a publisher to produce the book. This book is sold in bookstores and read in libraries as hard copies.

According to Wikipedia; Writing is a medium of human communication that involves the representation of a language through a system of physically inscribed, mechanically transferred or digitally represented symbols. Writing can also be said to be the art of using symbols (letters of the alphabets, punctuations and signs) to convey your thoughts, ideas or views in a readable form. Writing is not restricted to a set of people, it goes beyond race, religion, language or colour. Anyone can choose to write and express him or herself and also earn in the process. Writing goes farther than where the two legs of the writer could get to. So, through your writing your message can get to the end of the earth making a global impact. Your writing can create a huge traffic of followers for you around the globe thereby having more people believing in your cause, ideas and convictions. Your book(s) makes you an authority and a voice wherever you find yourself. A book is a legacy that outlives the writer. It also serves as a pool of knowledge and wisdom to its audience.

Through writing, the message of a writer echoes within globe, awakening the readers who never saw the author and may never see the author to the author's cause, dream, passion, ideas and creativity. Researchers have shown that the brain can engage in mental work like reading and writing effectively for two hours at a stretch, except in rare individual cases. When writing, to take a break after two stretch hours helps to keep the brain working. This is important, because, once the brain gets tired, the quality of its product on the subject matter in which it engages becomes watery and questionable. Also, to be able to write tangible and meaningful books, one needs to be a reading role model. You can neither be creative nor creatively write if you don't read. Reading opens the world to the reader and expands the horizon of the writer cum reader.

The art of writing books which enables individuals to share their thoughts on interested areas of their choice has existed for centuries. In the past, books were manually written (analogue) which was very tedious and took longer time to have published copies on book shelves. But, in recent years, book writing has taken a new dimension - the digital eBook revolution has made book writing simple and easier in meeting the aspirations and goals of the writer and also in meeting the needs of the targeted group. Such are the characteristics of highly priced books and bestsellers.

The essence of writing either eBook or manual books is to document an event in the past, present and future. There exist five major genres of writing. They are as follows:

1. Expository writing: This is referred to as informative writing. This writing aims to inform the reader of something. This type of writing tries to answer any question a reader might have on a particular issue or some issues. The writer should make this kind of writing as clear as possible and avoid technical jargons. Here, you share knowledge beyond doubts, or teach something to your audience.

2. Narrative writing: it tells a story. Narratives writing is written in chronological or non-chronological order and involves a variety of tenses. This is a basic form of storytelling and it shares something that happens to a character or an occurrence that took place in a vivid manner such that the audience will have detailed knowledge of the event.

3. Persuasive writing: This writing aims to persuade the readers of something. It usually makes use of personal pronouns and rhetorical questions. This is the idea of getting across to your audience an idea and convincing them to support and believe in your views.

4. Descriptive writing: This involves a detailed description of a place or person. This involves capturing every detail of what you are writing about; place, person, scene or thing. Here, you give full account of the features of a person, place or thing for quick and easy recognition.

5. Journal and Letter writing are among the oldest writing styles. It has drastically changed since the introduction of computers and smartphones. This style is usually written in the first person and is usually quite personal, especially in journal writing.

CHAPTER THREE

STRONG WRITING AND BESTSELLERS.

Strong writing is a writing that is captivating right from the start. It is the writing that captures the attention of its audience as a result of its style, language, imagery or the use of symbols and other rhetoric employed right from the start and holds the audience bounds until he finishes the whole book. Such stir up the curiosity of the reader and keeps him yearning for more until the very end of the story. In other words, strong writing should meet the need of your target audience, to the extent that they would be willing to pay for it or do anything to be in possession of your work. It should be targeted to solve a problem and not compound it. As we all know, people will pay a very high price for the knowledge they need to have their problem(s) solved. A strong title is very important in a book. It is not all the topics we have come with in our suggestions that we can get to other chapters. So, to help succeed in writing, let's look at five elements of good writing:

i. Purpose

ii. Audience

iii. Clarity

iv. Plot

v. Coherence

For a book to do well, it must be well written, articulated, purposeful, and STRONG. A strong book is a book which meets the need of the reader. It is considered strong because it holds the attention of the reader. It is a book which the reader would not want to put down unless he/she has finished reading. It is well written and compelling, goes beyond the literary needs. A strong writing which could make a strong book must contain the following:

1. It must be well written.
2. It must be compelling.
3. It must meet the needs of the reader.
4. It must contain a catchy title and forewords.
5. A strong book and a strong writing must give the reader the impression that you know and understand very well what you are writing about.

Strong writing or titles are produced through; (a) thorough and in-depth research; (b) having good reading skills; (c) working on grammar, syntax, and punctuation (get good editor and be willing to pay); (d) establish your audience and get into their mind by giving them what they cannot reject.

Strong books sells, people beg to buy them. They are best sellers.

WHAT ARE BESTSELLERS?

A published book can have the attribute called "bestselling" if the book has sold millions of copies, and is still in high demand. Bestselling books are books/publications that has the highest number of sold out copies in relation to other books in its category, within a given time frame. The sales can be far above 20,000 copies sold out within a specified period of time. What makes the book a bestseller is that it appeals to the reader, they get value, and keep buying it. Best sellers are carefully worked on by the authors by choosing a subject to write about, decides the type of medium to write in - is it going to be prose, poetry, or drama type of writing? Is it a research work? Will I write it in English, French or my local language, etc. After this, the writing commences and then when writing is concluded, the writer has to revise and check for mistakes, and effect corrections. The best of the best writing skill is put into the writing. The writer can even get a professional editor to look at the manuscript. All these processes lead to the book being a best seller. Above all, the writer has a particular audience in mind, and has to do some research, to be able to write well on the subject. Every writer has a passion for a particular idea or subject topic, and they go all the way to communicate it to the public. While writing therefore, there can be a roadblock when a writer needs to STOP writing. Note that stop here does not mean that a writer should give up writing, but for that particular project or for a short period of time. There are some moments or times when a writer can or may have to stop writing. Some of the reasons are:

1. When you feel like stopping
2. When writing becomes a struggle.
3. When u feel like increasing the content of your writing.

HOW TO WRITE A BESTSELLER

The authors of these bestsellers are called Best-selling authors. Very popular guys they are! I am sure we all here want to be bestselling authors smiling home with money in our pockets. A basic coach predecessor, Mrs Adetoun Adebisi OYELUDE listed the following tips for writing bestselling books and I when I read on how to do this, I found these tips to be top notch. The tips are as follows;

1. START WITH A BIG IDEA. BESTSELLERS ARE BUILT ON A BIG IDEA.

2. START IMMEDIATELY BECAUSE SOMEONE SOMEWHERE MIGHT HAVE THE SAME IDEA AS YOU DO.

3. BELIEVE THAT YOU HAVE SOMETHING VALUABLE TO SAY.

4. WRITE WITH THE AUDIENCE IN MIND. BESTSELLERS ARE STICKY.

5. CAPTURE THE READERS' ATTENTION WITH YOUR OPENING LINES.

6. BOOKWORM YOUR WAY TO SUCCESS (CULTIVATE THE HABIT OF READING i.e. BE A READING ROLE MODEL).

7. BE IN THE COMPANY OF LIKE MINDS. LIKE A WISE MAN WOULD SAY "SHOW ME YOUR FRIENDS AND I WILL TELL YOU WHO YOU ARE".

8. EDIT FOR CLARITY, NOT PERFECTION.

9. PACKAGE YOUR BOOK TO SPREAD (GREAT MARKETING STRATEGY LIES IN GOOD PACKAGING).

10. NEVER STOP LAUNCHING.

11. NEVER STOP TRYING, AND KEEP PUSHING

CHAPTER FOUR

A BOOK

Wikipedia defines a book as "a medium for recording information in the form of writing or images, typically composed of many pages bound together and protected by a cover". As an intellectual object, a book is prototypically a composition of such great length that it takes a considerable investment of time to read. In a restricted sense, a book is a self-sufficient section or part of a longer composition, a usage reflecting that, in antiquity, long works had to be written on several scrolls and each scroll had to be identified by the book it contained.

SECTIONS OF A BOOK

i. Cover page: This includes the title of the book and the author.

ii. Copyright page: The copyright page shows the author's name, year of publication and further warns against copyright infringement as thus: All Right Reserved. No part of this book should be used without the prior permission from the owner.

iii. Acknowledgement: This is where the writer appreciates those who in one way or the other contributed to the work.

iv. Table of Contents: This lists the chapters, topics and pages as it appears in the book. This gives the reader an insight of where to locate a particular chapter or topic.

v. Introduction: This briefly gives the reader an insight of what the book is all about.

vi. Body: Body is the content of the book. The writer should be able to prepare it to arouse the interest of the reader.

vii. Back page: The back page is divided into two and at the back cover of the book. The parts are: (a) About the author: The author gives the reader briefs about himself/ herself. The author's image is necessary. (b.) About the book: Here the author gives a summary description of the book.

CHAPTER FIVE

MS WORD

A word processor is a device or computer program that can be used to input, edit, and format a text, document, or file, often with additional features that aid such actions. Examples of word processors that can be used to create your e-book are Microsoft Word, Open Office writer, Google Drive document, WPS office writer, Word Perfect, and so on. The following is a guide on how to format your e-books using a customized template on Microsoft Word: Why Ms Word? You may ask. Well, Microsoft Word one word processing package that is very easy to use, and it is straightforward. Also, Ms Word offers several templates within the application from which you can choose a layout you wish to use in creating our books. Ms Word comes as a default writing tool with Ms Windows and can also be downloaded on other devices such as the mobile phones (from playstore). In essence, Ms Word aids stress-free and quality book creation and formatting.

PREPARING YOUR BOOK WITH MS WORD

There are two ways you can write your books using Ms Word;

1. Writing with the flow

You can start afresh while writing a new book, creating your own title page font, arrangement of table of contents and so on. As you do these, remember to follow a set standard.

2. By using a customised template. This might be your own template or someone else template.

The following are steps you can take while using a customized template to format your work;

- Open up the customized template on Ms Word.
- You'd see there are already written texts on the template.
- Set up your desired page and margin
- Trim your paper size (the universally accepted size is 6"×9". You can trip your paper size by clicking on page layout, then click on size, click on more page sizes, then adjust the paper size to 6"×9").
- To erase the existing texts and characters on the template, highlight all of them and click on your delete or backspace key.
- Choose suitable font styles and sizes you'd love to write in.
- You can now proceed with your placement of interiors (chapters and others).
- Fix in your title.
- Fix in your table of contents.

(You can choose to fix in your title and table of contents before you start writing or when you're done writing).

- Do your pagination (page numbering)
- Set your headers &footers
- Save your document to your device in preparation to upload it on the Amazon Kindle.

CHAPTER SIX

CREATING AN AMAZON KDP ACCOUNT

To be able to publish books on Amazon Kindle, you need to have an account on the Amazon KDP space. The following is a guide on how to create your Kindle Direct Publishing account on Amazon;

STEP BY STEP PROCESS!!!

1. Type the link kdp.amazon.com
2. Click on sign up
3. Click create account
4. Then verify your account
5. An OTP will be sent to your phone
6. Enter it
7. This would take you to a form where you need to fill your details. !!!!!!
8. Where you see postal code, please Google your Local Government code (the place you reside.) and fill it there.
9. Click save at the bottom right hand corner and then.
10. Complete Tax Information at the bottom left hand corner
11. Move to the next page and click individual at the top left hand
12. Click No

13. Fill your full name at the left and pick Country of citizenship at the right.

14. Remove the click on the box of I have a Non-US TIN and the "I have a U.S. TIN", it will take you to:

Why are you not able to provide a TIN?

15. Pick option 3 -I could not/have not obtained TIN from my local authorities because of other reasons

16. Move on and click I certify that I have the capacity...

17. Move to Signature and type your full name

18. Click save and preview

19. Click submit form20. Click exit interview

Then go to the top of the page and click Bookshelf to upload your manuscript.

Click individual and fill all other information

CHAPTER SEVEN

FORMATTING

Formatting is arranging your papers in an understandable form until submitting them for publication. It is involved with the proper design of the article before it is printed. Formatting helps in preparing your electronic book for Publishing. It set up the document to meet an acceptable publishing standard. In the digital publishing world, it means presenting your book in an acceptable format for publishing by using proper paragraphs. There are two types of formatting to consider in this case: basic and advanced. When learning, one should always begin with the basics before progressing to the advanced.

Using a customised template to format your eBook, we edit what is on the template and copy and paste our lecture notes into chapters. The basic template for use is the Create Space 6" x 9". Copy and paste your manuscript into this template, or begin typing. Before using, remove any existing text. The book can be divided into the following:

Title

Author Name

Copyright

Acknowledgement

Contents

Chapters

About the Author.

The above description is a manual form of Formatting manuscript for a beginner.

The advanced formatting style is more professional than the previous chapter's basic style. This advanced type transforms your work using an app. The app is named KINDLE CREATE APP. The steps for using the Kindle Create are as follows:

(1) Download the Kindle Create App from Amazon's KDP store.

(2) Install the application on a Windows 64-bit PC.

(3) Run the application, and

(4) Select the unformatted document from your computer to import it.

(5) Fill out the front and back matter with the necessary information.

(6) Choose a theme to style the manuscript;

(7) Place the cursor on Chapter One;

(8) Click Insert and Table of Contents to generate the table of contents.

(9) Highlight and style the first paragraph, then repeat for the remaining ones.

(10) Save the manuscript in the kpf package.

(11) Examine and publish the eBooks.

CHAPTER EIGHT

EBOOK AND PAPERBACK

Simply put, E-Book means Electronic Book, Book is writing and publishing through electronic media/medium instead of hard copy or as an extension of the hard copy to reach a wider audience. It is a book in electronic format that is not physically handled. It is prepared, made available and accessible by electronic means and computer and related devices or technology. It can either be accessed online or offline. EBooks can be in different formats, which includes:

1. EPUB
2. AZW
3. PDF

Most common eBooks platforms are: Amazon, Barnes and Noble & Google play. In this book, our focus is on Amazon.

ADVANTAGES OF EBOOK

The following are some of the benefits of e-books:

- They save space
- They save money
- They save the environment
- They can be downloaded instantly

- The font sizes can be changed.
- They can be searched for easily

HOW TO WRITE AN EBOOK

1. Define your objectives - why are you writing the book and who are you writing it for? (This will help you choose a good title)

2. Outline the book into introduction, chapters and others.

3. While writing, include details and be creative (note that some e-books have low contents like colouring books and planners).

4. When you are done writing, proof read your work.

5. Convert (upload), publish and promote the e-book. Amazon KDP accepts MS Word; MS Word is the application we should use to save our manuscript documents.

CHAPTER NINE

KINDLE CREATE APP

Kindle create helps you format your kindle e-book much easily without have to go through the manual and time consuming traditional formatting procedure. The app can however not function effectively on a mobile phone.

HOW TO DOWNLOAD THE KINDLE CREATE APP

1. Log on to your KDP app

2. Scroll down and click on the hyperlink text "get started with kindle content creator tools"

3. It will take you to the kindle tools and resources. When you are there, on the manuscript formatting resources session, scroll down and underneath the schematic image, you would see several options. Click on the Kindle Create.

4. You would be directed to the amazon page, where you would be given two options either to download Kindle Create on PC or on MAC. Click on any of the download options as it applies to you.

HOW TO USE KINDLE CREATE APP

If you follow the steps below on how to use the Kindle create app to prepare a well- formatted manuscript that would be ready for publication. You will start with an unformatted manuscript and end with a well formatted manuscript that is ready for publication

1. When you open your kindle create app, click on "Choose" and then click "choose the file" and select the file you want to work on.

2. The file would be imported and converted into the Kindle create app. Depending on the volume of your book it may take some time before it can completely import and convert the manuscript.

3. Click on continue to start formatting your book.

NOTE: Once your book has been properly formatted it would give you a table of content which you can either accept or reject.

4. On the left side of the page there is a section called contents which consists of the front matter, body and back matter

5. Click on the "plus sign" beside the front matter it would bring out the

Title page

Copyright

Dedication

Epigraph

Table of contents

Preface

Introduction

Prologue

Foreword

Standard page (Front matter)

Click on desired options and fill in the details appropriately.

6. Just like the front matter, click on the "plus sign" beside the back matter it would bring out the following options

Books by the author

About the author

Epilogue

Afterword

Acknowledgement

Click on desired options and fill in the details appropriately

7. On the right upper corner of the page there are several icons that you would use to further format your manuscript.

➢ Print settings: here you set how you want your headings and the interior of how to book to appear.

➢ Theme: this allows you to choose the style of writing you want your book to be in. by default it is in the modern theme but you can change it to either classic, cosmos or armor.

➢ Save: just like you save in Microsoft word.

➢ Preview: you can see how far you have gone with your book creation. You can also see how it would look on a tablet and other devices.

➢ Publish: this is the last stage of your book formatting after you are done formatting click on publish. The formatted document will be saved in the file where the original document was saved, but it will save the file as a KPF file.

8. At the right side of your page, there is a section with which you can format the text properties. Whatever you do to this right side will affect the section on the left side of the page. This however works in relation to the position of your cursor. This makes formatting easy and enjoyable.

9. Once your manuscript is already well-formatted, to get your table of content move up to the first chapter of your manuscript and put your cursor before the first chapter title and move your mouse to the insert icon on the left upper corner of the page and then click on table of content to generate a table of content.

10. At the end of these, click on publish.

Note: the ISBN issued by the Kindle create app is the default ISBN. Replace it with the ISBN you were assigned on your KDP account. The Kindle Create app ISBN comes with two ISBNs, one 10-digit and the other 13- digit. Delete both and replace them with the one you were given on your KDP account.

KPD/KCB VERSUS KDP PDF PREVIEW PROOF COPY

KPF OR KCB would be generated after formatting using the kindle create software while KDP PDF preview proof copy would be generated after uploading your KPF/KCB files on your kdp.amazon.com account during the PUBLISHING of your paperback only!!

DIFFERENCE BETWEEN THE KPF FILE AND PDF FILE

1. After formatting your manuscripts with your Kindle create software, it converts it to a KPF file.

2. It is the KPF file you'd be expected to upload on your kdp.amazon.com account as your manuscript.

3. During the publishing of your paperback, upon uploading the KPF file. During the preview, it is at that point you're to download you'd KDP PDF preview proof copy.

4. You cannot view the KPF file - it can only be read by the KDP software.

After publishing, your paperback will come live in 2-3 days.

CHAPTER TEN
ISBN

ISBN is International Standard Book Number. It is the national standard number for uniquely identifying books. ISBN helps customers identify and order the exact book they want to purchase on Amazon. With the KDP publishing process, you have the option of using your own ISBN procured from your country or you can request for a free ISBN. Using the free ISBN is advantageous because amazon KDP may not recognize the one gotten from your country and this may limit the distribution of your book. The KDP ISBN cannot be used outside Amazon KDP. ISBN is not required when publishing e-book.

HOW TO GET YOUR FREE ISBN

✓ Log in to your KDP account.

✓ Go to your bookshelf.

✓ Start the KDP paperback publishing process.

✓ Fill the details until you get to the ISBN page, here it would ask you if you want the KDP free ISBN or not.

CHAPTER ELEVEN

CREATING A FOREIGN BANK ACCOUNT

There are two ways by which you can receive your royalties from amazon. The first way is through the use of cheque and the second way is through transfer. If you choose to be paid with cheque, a physical cheque will be sent to the address you filled on your Amazon KDP account during your account opening process which can now be cashed at your bank. But choosing the transfer option, you will have to open a foreign account with the options: Payoneer, PayPal, etc. It is this that brought us to the opening of a Payoneer account because this method of receiving money is faster, easier, and more convenient. With it, the money you made from Royalties can be easily transferred to your local bank within a little time or withdrawn at any ATM stand.
To open such account, follow the procedures below:

1. Type www.payoneer.com on your browser

2. Click register

3. Select the appropriate option from the drop-down box (individual)

4. Then select "get paid by international clients or market places".

5. Then click register

For the first interface, fill in the following information

1. Name

2. Surname
3. Email address
4. Re-enter Email address
5. Date of birth
6. Then click next

For second the next interface fill in the following details

1. Country of Residence
2. Address
3. Zip Code
4. Mobile Number
5. Verification Code sent to your mobile number

For the third interface, fill in the following details

1. Your email address
2. Your password
3. Re-enter password
4. Your security (2) questions
5. Your security (2) answers
6. Your ID or passport Number
7. Date of issue
8. Date of expiration
9. Random decode selection

For the fourth and final interface, fill in the following details

1. Your bank name
2. Your bank number
3. Indicate if it is cheque or savings
4. Swift code. And your registration is done.

Once created, click on the USD option to capture the bank details that will be uploaded to kindle direct publishing.

The details are the following

1. Bank Name
2. Band Address
3. Routing
4. Account Number Domiciled
5. Account Type
6. Reference Name

You will then launch your kindle direct publishing account and provide the details such as name of the bank domiciled in the US with the address, account type, account number and reference in the portion interface responsible for payment. After updating your details, you will receive a successful prompt which indicates that you have provided all the required information. You will now process to provide the details of your tax income number referred to TIN.

If your country's TIN is accepted by Kindle Direct Publishing, you can input it but when it does not accept your country of residence TIN, you must give a reason it is not acceptable. Once you have filled all the information required in the TIN section, your account will be given the go ahead to publish your books do the pricing

NOTE: Remember, payoneer acts as the intermediary bank between the US and your local bank. And that is why it is extremely important to get this right information.

REFERENCES

Ati, O.F. (2022). Lecture Note.

Dima, R. M. (2022). Introduction to E-Book creation and publishing

KDP Build Your Book – Format a Paperback Manuscript (2018). Copyright © 2018 Amazon.com, Inc. or its affiliates. All rights reserved.

Kindle Add-In for Microsoft Word User Guide. Version 0.97 Beta, (2017).

Write-for-me (2022). Lecture Note and videos.

ACKNOWLEDGEMENT

I wish to acknowledge Almighty Allah for His grace and infinite mercy, my mum, siblings, husbands and my wonderful children for their understanding and unwavering support throughout this sojourn. I will love to specially say a big THANK YOU to OGAPATAPTA for taking me through this redefining adventure.

ABOUT THE AUTHOR

Nasirat Imran

She is a graduate of Yoruba Language and Literature of Obafemi Awolowo University, Ile-Ife, Osun State, Nigeria. A realist and a potential researcher.

www.ingramcontent.com/pod-product-compliance
Lightning Source LLC
LaVergne TN
LVHW052111160826
845678LV00015B/3485

* 9 7 9 8 3 5 1 3 2 7 9 2 1 *